Gabriel Dumont Speaks

Gabriel Dumor

translated by Michael Barnholden

Talonbooks • Vancouver • 1993

published with the assistance of The Canada Council

Talonbooks
201 / 1019 East Cordova Street
Vancouver, British Columbia
Canada V6A 1M8

Typeset in Palatino. Printed and bound in Canada by Hignell Printing Ltd.

First printing: March 1993

Canadian Cataloguing in Publication Data

Dumont, Gabriel, 1837-1906.
Gabriel Dumont speaks

ISBN 0-88922-323-8
1. Dumont, Gabriel, 1837-1906. 2. Riel Rebellion, 1885—Personal narrative. 3. Métis—Canada, Western—Biography. I. Barnholden, Michael, 1951- II. Title.
FC3217.1.D84A3 1993 971.05'4'092
F1060.9.D84A3 1993 C93-091209-8

National Archives of Canada, Ottawa (Photo No. A8211)

Possibly Madeline Dumont with Gabriel Dumont

Introduction

Gabriel Dumont was born in what is now Winnipeg in 1837 or 1838, fourth of the eleven children (five girls and six boys) of Isidore Dumont and Louise Laframboise. Isidore was the head of the Dumont band, inheriting that position from his father, Jean Baptiste Dumont, who had come west from Quebec in the 1790s and married a Sarcee woman. When Gabriel was two, his father decided to leave the farm where he had three acres under cultivation, for the life of an independent trader in the Fort Pitt area. Gabriel's childhood was spent moving back and forth across the prairie following the hunt and learning the skills associated with that life.

In 1858 Gabriel Dumont met and married Madeline Welkey, daughter of a Scottish trader and his Indian wife. He began to fashion a life based on his hunting prowess. Because the hunt took him from the Red River to the foot of the Rockies, he always did a little trading on the side. His hunting travels brought him in contact with the Blackfoot, Sioux, and Crow, and he became conversant in all their languages. At the time he was elected chief of the band in 1863, the Dumonts were using the Batoche area as a winter camp, and by 1868 the decision was made to move and settle there permanently.

As head of the Dumont band Gabriel presided over the hunt, negotiated peace treaties, and formed alliances with other prairie nations. As more and more settlers took up homesteads, commercial activity grew, the territorial government became increasingly active, and Dumont's leadership took on a political and diplomatic role, culminating in his election as president of the short-lived St. Laurent council in December of 1873. Diplomacy does not seem to have been his favourite aspect of the job, as his patience with government bureaucracies was short at best. Following the hunt, trading a little, hauling some freight, even guiding missionaries took care of his material needs quite nicely. For Dumont to abandon that way of life was simply asking too much.

But daily the Métis were being asked to do just that. The circumstances forcing them to take up land, farm, pay for wood cut on crown land and give up the hunt inevitably led to the end of their nomadic way of life. Dumont eventually got title to the property where the south branch of the Carlton Trail crossed the South Saskatchewan River, opened a small store, and operated a scow ferry at what came to be known as Gabriel's Crossing. It has been said that Madeline, who could read and write as well as speak English, taught school at Batoche in the years before the "rebellion." By the summer of 1884, when the Métis asked Louis Riel to return to negotiate their grievances, Dumont's modest wealth could be measured by the slate billiard table which took up most of his store, and the hand-cranked washing machine that eased the domestic burden of his household.

Dumont confirms his now legendary offer to "bring the Indians" to reinforce Riel's army at Red River in the "rebellion" of 1869. Although this present text seems to indicate that Riel did not know Dumont very well if at all, before 1884, it remains a possibility that the offer was made through intermediaries. During the 1885 "rebellion," Riel appointed Dumont adjutant general in charge of the army of the new nation of the Northwest. The two men differed over tactics and religion, yet Dumont loyally supported the basic ideal Riel espoused — the Métis as a free and independent nation — and fought long and hard for it. After Riel surrendered in May of 1885, Dumont fled to the United States, hoping to organize further resistance and possibly a jail break for Riel. Madeline died of tuberculosis shortly after joining him in Montana. Close to fifty of the Métis men died during the war, others were arrested, and many more fled either north to wilder country, or south to the U.S.A.

Riel was hung in November of 1885, and the following spring Dumont joined Buffalo Bill's Wild West show, where he was billed as "the Hero of the Halfbreed Rebellion." He stayed with the show until shortly after his pardon in the summer of 1886, after which he took on speaking engagements before French-speaking audiences in the northeastern States. In late 1887 and early 1888, he was brought to Quebec to help with Honoré Mercier's election campaign, which had as one of its central issues recriminations concerning Riel's hanging. However, Dumont again soon tired of politics and public speaking, and returned to the Wild West Show, performing as a marksman and outrider for a brief period before heading back west to a cabin on a relative's property, to resume a life of hunting, fishing, and trapping.

A photo taken close to this time, in approximately 1900, shows him to be a large man in his sixties wearing a rough suit and vest. His watch chain is draped from a button down to his vest pocket, and two medals are prominent on his chest. He wears a fine black Stetson and carries an ornately carved cane. The once full beard is now trimmed and his chin is bare, but he still wears his riding boots. In six years he will be dead.

◆ ◆ ◆

If the Métis had been regarded as a nation similar to the other tribes on the prairie, but as separate and distinct as the Cree or the Sioux to whom they were closely related, post-contact events would have been seen in a very different light. However, the Métis were in fact an entirely unique people in the history of the colonization of the Americas, whose culture, values and politics were a synthesis of native plains people, and the second wave of white, usually franco-phone colonials who arrived on the praires after the first wave of explorers. This second wave of colonials were for the most part, fur trade workers, often little more than indentured servants to the Hudson's Bay Company or the Northwest Company, some of whom chose to remain on the prairie. Intermarriage with these new immigrants became a common practice among most of the great Plains tribes, particularly the Cree. When the White fur traders came to the west in the 1700s, those who wished to stay were welcomed, and very quickly large bands of mixed bloods became a third culture on the prairies, creating a distinct culture which was a hybrid between the encroaching White andthe retreating Indian cultures. The Métis soon became leaders in the resistance to the cultural and corporate invasion led by the Church, the fur trade companies and the C.P.R.

The Métis and other mixed bloods created their culture by borrowing elements from a variety of languages and cultures and adapting them to suit their needs. In fact, the Métis of the Batoche area probably spoke a form of incipient Michif, a dialect using Cree sentence structure and verb forms and French nouns. Cree was the first language of the Dumont band. Most of those tried after the War who could be said to be members of the Dumont band elected to be tried in Cree. Thus, while it can be said that Métis culture was syncretic in essence, there is no question that its predominant elements were native.

The social organization of the Métis tribe must therefore be compared to that of its neighbouring and related tribes, rather than to those of either English or French

National Archives of Canada, Ottawa (photo no. C-5817)

Gabriel Dumont around 1900

tribes, rather than to those of either English or French Canada. By the mid-1800s, and possibly earlier, there were at least two distinct Métis cultures: the settled Métis, and the "wild" or free Métis of the Plains, who chose to leave the Red River rather than settle down. By 1884 the Métis were far from a homogeneous culture. There were those who lived in two-storey houses, working as freighters and traders, those who lived in tipis and subsisted on the hunt, and still others who had become treaty Indians. Some worked for the government as agricultural instructors, (although very few Métis were farmers), or as clerks and interpreters.

Métis life was originally based on sharing vast areas of public land as needed. But the buffalo hunt gradually ended, the last one leaving Batoche in 1882, and returning with only eleven animals. It is important to note that as long as the buffalo remained plentiful, the Métis adopted Indian ways on the hunt and in the winter camps, while preserving some of the ways of their French forefathers at their home bases in settlements such as Red River and Batoche. Land was preempted in the settlements on the basis of French river lots, although actual title was not obtained until later, when government regulations came into force. This system conflicted with the Canadian system of surveying on a grid, and had created a problem in Red River, as it would later on the South Saskatchewan. As the land base began to shrink, and the buffalo disappeared, the Métis culture was forced to change. Eventually a broad-based political consensus developed, having as its main concern land tenure for all residents of the Northwest — Métis, Indians, mixed bloods, and other settlers, including the English of the Prince Albert district. Under the leadership of Dumont and others, petitions were presented to both the appointed territorial government and the federal government in Ottawa. No replies were forthcoming. It seems clear to me that the Métis were willing to negotiate by treaty, nation to nation. Riel wrote to Sir John A. MacDonald informing him that Dumont was angry that every minor chief but him had been offered a treaty. When all their petitions and representations failed, the Métis called upon Riel to negotiate with the government.

Riel was an educated, settled Métis who had negotiated a treaty, nation to nation, with the new country of Canada in 1870, an accomplishment that caused him to be seen as the Social Chief of the Métis. Dumont, on the other hand, was seen as a "wild" Métis, chief of his band, and for his feats was accorded the status of War Chief. This delegation of roles parallels the relative positions taken by the Cree's Big Bear and Wandering Spirit. Having learned from his previous experience in Manitoba, Riel saw force as a threat to further negotiations with Canada, but when the negotiations proved ineffective, the War Chief took over. The horse, the rifle, even sticks and stones became the weapons of the tribe in its battle with the government of Canada only after all negotiations had ended unsuccessfully. The individual warrior was free to follow either chief, as far as he wished. It is clear from Dumont's account, however, that the Métis fought in the manner of the Indians.

Dumont saw war through Indian eyes, and not from the perspective of the then very "modern" major general Frederick Middleton, veteran of many English campaigns and the commander of the Canadian forces during the "rebellion." Short, quick engagements, often executed at night by a highly mobile force that knew the country well — essentially guerrilla tactics — was probably the only strategy the Métis could have used to hold their ground for a time against the untried, hastily gathered Canadian troops. What surprised the Métis was the large number of white men, well-equipped with guns, food, and transportation, who were put in the field, and the length of time they were prepared simply to sit and wait. I believe Riel was well aware of the long term limitations of the Métis strategy, and therefore logically preferred negotiations. His record of past conciliatory success allowed him to overrule Dumont's instincts, temporarily.

◆ ◆ ◆

During his speaking tour of Quebec in 1887 and 1888, Dumont dictated his first memoir of the "Riel Rebellion" to a group of journalists and politicians. His story was taken down by B.A.T. Montigny, the recorder for Quebec City. The dictation was read back to him one month later for his approval and, after being edited by Adolphe Ouimet, was privately published as part of *La Verité sur la Question Métisse au Nord-Ouest* (1889). The book, long out of print, is a polemic that was used to advance the fortunes of the Quebec Liberal Party.

G.F.G. Stanley translated this first Dumont memoir into English in the 1949 issue of the *Canadian Historical Review* — an obscure publication, perhaps, but not so arcane as to be unavailable in the libraries of any large Canadian city. It is extensively quoted in almost every work on Riel and any aspect of the "rebellion."

Dumont's second memoir, published here for the first time, was dictated in 1903, probably in the confines of some friend's parlour, over drinks and food, and definitely lacks the overt political agenda tacked on to the first dictation of 1888. This second memoir was also delivered eighteen years after the main events described therein actually occurred. Until now, no one has published or translated the second dictation, and it is seldom referred to in the literature on the Métis experience.

We have in these two dictations one person's account of the same events given in two radically different circumstances — the one a self-conscious delivery for an audience whose agenda Dumont probably was little concerned with and may not even have known, the other a raw, unmediated version. He was requested to give the first dictation solely because of his connection to Riel, and he was apparently promptly dropped as a potential political ally of the Quebec Liberal Party when his anti-clerical stance became known. When we compare the edited history with the later, more private account, we discover discrepancies between the two that manifest a dichotomy of belief — a comfortable acceptance of officially-sanctioned history versus a deep-rooted suspicion that we can't believe everything we read, particularly if it is endorsed by the authorities. This second text presents the history of the vanquished, and urges us to question the received version of history by allowing us to see what happened from the other side.

The most obvious and insistent difference between this oral history and the accepted version of the Métis' story lies in Dumont's views on the "rebellion." He saw it not as a French revolt against English Canadian authority, but rather as a War between two nations — one an indigenous people, with broad local support, fighting to repel the other: an uncompromising, overwhelming invader that was insensitive and totally unresponsive to the concerns of the people it had assumed the authority to govern. Today this War may seem like the act of a desperate, deluded people. But it was a war fought between two armies so disparate they did not share even basic assumptions about what war was, or why they were fighting. Only Indians could win a war fought using Indian tactics, and only the whites could win a European-style war, and Dumont knew this.

◆ ◆ ◆

The original manuscripts of Dumont's 1903 dictations, which I have treated as one complete manuscript, are now held in the archive of L'Union Nationale Métisse de Saint-Joseph in the Manitoba Provincial Archives. They consist of 104 handwritten pages, of the same size for the most part, although at least two pages have been ripped from other smaller sources. A quill pen was used, and the handwriting appears to belong to one person. The identity of the transcriber is not known. The dictation may have been done on more than one occasion, perhaps on two consecutive evenings: there are two page ones, but neither is the first page. The first twelve pages serve as an introduction, and reflect the evening's preliminaries: a small group had gathered, opening remarks were made, questions asked and answered, and the tone of the narrative was set. The handwriting is cramped, suggesting that the writer was rushing to keep up with Dumont's speech. The most awkward part of the transcription is the way the recorder chose to handle the narrative. Dumont must have spoken in the first person, but the narrative is written in the third person. It is my opinion that French, the transcriber's first language, was Dumont's second or third. The text refers to his ability to speak Cree and Sioux, and implies he knew Blackfoot. He may have delivered this dictation in what linguists refer to as incipient Michif. The syntax is certainly not typically French, but there seem to be no Cree words. Perhaps the transcriber also spoke Michif and rendered it into his torturous French as he wrote. It seems most likely that some language difference between the transcriber and Dumont made the task of transcribing exceedingly difficult.

I came into possession of my copy of the manuscript about twenty years ago through a case of mistaken identity. I had requested a photocopy of the "Dumont Dictation" from the National Archives of Canada. I thought I was asking for the 1887 dictation but the version I was sent was clearly a different text. I translated about half of it and used the material for an epic poem that I eventually abandoned. Yet something kept pulling me back to the text. My experience working for Talonbooks on *Write it on Your Heart* with Wendy Wickwire and Harry Robinson taught me that the way to deal with the Dumont text was really very simple: let him speak. A direct, literal translation would be of little use except to scholars, so I have made what I call an interpretation. I see my work as interpreter resembling that of the Métis interpreters, and others such as Peter Erasmus, who also translated words coming from a very different time and place, and tried to pass them on to a contemporary world. I am also aware that this work may have considerable impact in today's Métis culture, which is as factionalized, and as capable of dealing with their differences, as any other society. I am not so naive as to think that different organizations will not use Dumont's memoirs in ways consistent with their own biases. However, it is my hope that Dumont's words can make a valuable contribution to the contemporary discourse on a variety of important subjects, rather than serve narrow political agendas. There is, of course, always room for error, in this method, not so much in the meaning of the words, but in the cultural context of those words. I tried, however, not to tamper with what was said, but have changed awkward sentence structures, usually by making two short sentences out of one long one. I have also restored the first person in order to let the narrative move in the natural manner of a man telling his story to friends, with the ease and comfort that came with eighteen years of telling his story. I hope my interpretation does Dumont's story the justice that it deserves.

This document preserves an unrepeatable oral event, and offers us the rare opportunity to view one of the central events in the history of the Métis, as perceived by one of their key heroes. The War has of course been much-documented by the dominant culture, but its historians rely primarily on written sources, and largely ignore the contributions of oral historians like Dumont. In an oral culture, history is passed from generation to generation, often by a singer or teller who inherits or is elected to that position. There are ancient, traditional myths and legends whose particular rhythms and phrasing would probably not alter much even through generations of retellings. But oral history is not static, and new stories would be added to account for environmental and societal changes. And what are those paintings on tipis? What are those rock effigies, petroglyphs, cave paintings, totems, masks, and other intentionally and elaborately designed objects but an oral culture's library — the records of its cosmology, religion, tribal, and clan histories. Unfortunately, "oral culture" is too often equated with "illiterate," and therefore "backward," culture. Together with "oral history," terms like "primitive" and "aboriginal" are frequently used derogatorily, while "literate," "developed" and "civilized" are privileged by a dominant culture that somehow deems itself superior by virtue of its print-dependency. When a dominant culture demands cultural conformity, it simultaneously sets out to erase cultural difference. In this method of disempowerment lie the germs of cultural genocide. The only possible response left is resistance, and the record of that resistance becomes the strength and heart of this necessary cultural struggle.

Gabriel Dumont recited his own — and Métis — history with great dignity. He was an old warrior telling tales of bravery and daring, speaking from his heart, unconcerned with conforming to established "truth." Both his story, and the opportunity to tell it, mattered to him. I believe that he would have wanted this piece widely disseminated, without its integrity being violated. Yet this document, which I believe to be in the public domain, has languished for ninety years, and is only now being made public, only in translation. The implicit challenge to his listeners, and now his readers, is to open our ears and eyes so that his difference may be accepted.

Historically, this text is interesting on a number of counts, not the least of which is its never having been published before. It is referred to in some of the material on Dumont, Riel and the War of 1885, but not always, and certainly not consistently. Often, quotations from this dictation are excerpted but their source is unacknowledged, or they become secondary references that are not properly attributed. In addition, this second dictation seems to have been confused with the first at times. Why most historians have chosen not to acknowledge the 1903 document is puzzling, unless we consider how it would fit into the received version of history. The 1887 dictation slotted quite neatly into an electoral political agenda, and thus is useful for historical research that continues to serve similar purposes — in no way does it contradict the official historical record. The second dictation, however contradicts or certainly questions much of what is popularly believed about the Métis and their "rebellion."

The validity and reliability of oral history have long been disputed. But recently, history has been recognized to be a variable and multifaceted process, rather than an unmoving, monolithic Truth. The consequence of this rupture in history's hermetic seal is an acceptance of diverse writings and voices that defy the authorized-document fetish, and challenge the tyranny of "official" sources. The responsibility of telling history is thus restored to the public domain, where it belongs. This text contains a moving example that raises the issue in a somewhat different way: Dumont's claim that the Canadian troops used explosive bullets against the Métis, is one I have never seen before, in any work on the "rebellion." In the tradition of written history, this kind of revision would be considered "true" if enough of a documentable paper trail could be amassed to successfully alter the "facts". This type of evidence, however, is absent — by definition — in an oral culture, and consequently the revised histories that emerge in such a tradition are regarded with suspicion by historians relying on printed proof: they are considered to be mutable, open to improvised "improvements" and therefore, false. But this assumption ignores two possible circumstances that can account for such revisions. First, the oral historian can discover new corroborating evidence relayed by others — data as important to the oral historian's process of gathering information as signed and witnessed documents are to that of print-fixated the historian. Second, the "new" evidence provoking a revision may have been withheld intentionally, thus precluding earlier acess to it.

This second dictation is a much more politically trenchant text than the first because of the way it unsettles the existing historical record. Over one hundred years later, the issues raised by Dumont have not been addressed by any Canadian government. When Gabriel Dumont speaks we listen, and we can hear eerie echoes between his story and the recent crisis at Oka. We continue to ignore this history at our peril.

◆ ◆ ◆

Gabriel Dumont Speaks

After Batoche, Father Andre said to the police, "you are looking for Gabriel? Well, you are wasting your time, there isn't a blade of grass on the prairie he does not know."

I did not want to surrender. I asked those who were surrendering to give me their bullets. I got eighty for my rifle and forty for my gun. I took the revolver from the sheriff, gave it to Monkman and then took it back again. I wanted Riel to cross the line with me. I looked for him every day for four days. One time I called him from a bluff thinking he might be nearby. And that's right where he was — with the women and Nicolas Fageron, who recognized my voice. Riel thought it might be an English trap and would not answer.

Moise Ouellette took a letter from Middleton for Riel and me, asking us to surrender and promising us justice. Ouellette found me but I told him I would not surrender. Then he asked me where Riel was, and I said "I am looking for him too, but *I* want to help him escape."

The fourth evening I encountered Ouellette again. He had lost his horse and asked me for one. "Well, that's strange," I answered. "You want me to give my horse to someone who now works for the government?" Not on your life! But all the same, I did direct him to the families camped near Bellevue who might give him a horse.

The fourth day Riel gave himself up. When I heard about it I decided to leave by myself. I camped that night with Jean Dumont. I said my goodbyes and left. As I rode away someone yelled. It was Michel Dumas and he wanted to go with me. I thought about it and said he could come. Then he drank away the money given us by our American friends and lost their support.

During the four days I spent around Batoche I did not go past Bellevue, about eight or ten miles away. Meanwhile, the plains were covered by enemy patrols looking for me. Each night I would camp at Batoche, and the next day I would wait for the patrols to leave and follow behind them. The whole day I was right behind them. From time to time I would stop on a bluff and wait while they scouted around, then I would go on. I knew the country like the back of my hand, I knew where they would stop and where I would not be seen, so I just stayed right behind them while they searched. I had decided never to be taken alive. "I will never fall into their hands," I thought. I counted on my skill with horse and rifle and my cold blooded will.

◆ ◆ ◆

People thought that Riel surrendered in the end to save the lives of those who had fought with him, that he offered himself in their place. He thought they would be happy with his head. Once during this time he said to his wife, "oh my poor Marguerite, I know the Good Lord wants me to die." Riel had also said before that "if it turns bad and the leaders are saved, there will be many followers who are lost." In prison he said "I know that I will be pardoned by God, but not by men. Gabriel will be pardoned by both God and men."

Another time in prison, Riel was enlarging a hole he had found in the wooden door. As Joseph Delorme passed on his way to the toilet, Riel said to him, "when you come back, go slowly and do not look at me. I have something to ask you." Riel then asked him "do you know where Dumont is?" He told Riel that I had crossed the line. "Good," said Riel." That will be good for all of you. You will go on living, but not me. You can depend on Dumont. He will travel all over, and be well received everywhere he goes, and give great service to our people. I am going to die but he will live to a ripe old age."

Joseph Delorme, now at Dauphin, lost both testicles at the battle of Batoche. The bullet also went through his thigh. He was found and looked after by the English. There were huge flaps of skin on both sides of the wound. To close it, the women put him on a table and wanted to put him to sleep. He refused, and laughed while they operated to show he had no fear.

Michel Dumas and I surrender to the American Police

When we got to Fort Assiniboine we went at once to the authorities. We were put in the hands of a sergeant who made us follow him. He took us down a long hall and opened a door which led to a cell, made us go in, and locked the door behind us.

"Well," I laughed, "this will be just fine. At least we don't have to sleep outside."

Very shortly the sergeant returned, quickly opened the door and made us come out, excusing himself because, he said, he had made a mistake. He was not supposed to put us in there but instead he was supposed to put us in the best room, and he took us there. We stayed there after that, with an officer to wait on us and make new excuses.

Next we were taken to the Fort's superior officer who spoke French. He told us he was going to telegraph the government about our case right away. While we stayed there we were well-treated. The message to set us free came at two in the morning on the third day.

At the end we had about seventy rifles to fight the English. A Frenchman, Paul Chelet, went to their camp and talked to an English officer, asking if he knew how many had been killed by their machine gun.

"No? Well I do," Chelet said.

"How many then? I would like to know."

"Well, just one."

"No — that's not possible."

"Yes, and it was my horse."

The officer was so mad he wanted to hit Chelet. He knew he would be mocked by the others.

◆ ◆ ◆

When Riel heard mass he would always say, "Quick! Quickly — ask for God's pardon."

One day he said this to a Métis who answered him, "well, he never listens to me."

"That does not matter," said Riel. "You must not offend the Good Lord. You must ask. He will hear you and answer your prayers. So beg His pardon and mine as well."

"Pardon."

"You must take mass from only me."

Some of the priests were becoming impatient because Riel was discouraging the people from taking mass. Riel told them not to love the priests because they did not follow the law of God. "They only want to convert the world to make money," he told them.

◆ ◆ ◆

Between Duck Lake and Fish Creek, Riel spoke to a meeting at the church one day.

"We must kill the English prisoners."

There had been a man in their care and they let him fall out of bed. Another time Antoine Vandal had nearly lost his head and he begged me, "cousin, I do not want to die." He was crawling after me, begging me.

The Arrest of Monkman after the Battle of Duck Lake

Riel said one day, "I have dreamed that there is a traitor among us and he wants to desert."

Then he said to me, "In my dream the traitor was a short one."

So it had to be Monkman. I also remembered the day we went to scout out on the other side of the crossroads near Duck Lake, and he was not where he was supposed to be. So he could have been the traitor.

"I know that two of them have been asked to betray us. I want to know who they are and who asked them to desert," Riel said, and he asked me to call all the people together. So I called everyone together and did as Riel asked. But no one had been asked.

As far as Riel was concerned, Monkman was guilty. So we arrested him and put him in the basement of Boyer's house beside his store. The other prisoners were free in the room, but Monkman was chained by the leg up through the floor and around a small joist.

When we went to arrest Monkman he tried to defend himself. He went for his revolver. I threw myself in front of the men who were trying to arrest him and grabbed his gun telling him I would kill him if he moved. Monkman was scared and surrendered. I disarmed him, taking back the revolver I had given him before.

◆ ◆ ◆

Between Fish Creek and Batoche, my wife and Old Batoche cared for the wounded. One day Riel sent Jackson and the police prisoners to Duck Lake for safekeeping. When the Indians there saw them go by they wanted their police scarves, and it was all I could do to hold them back.

Cardinal died. He went mad first. Old Batoche found a piece of bone from his fractured skull in his pillow. We thought that the English prisoners had let some of the wounded die. I told Riel right then that the lives of the English prisoners were worth nothing, and they could no longer be trusted to care for the wounded.

A Sioux took care of the rifles at Batoche. He was very good at it. Jim Levace made bullets with the lead from tea cases. The captains were William Boyer, Isidore Dumont, Augustin Laframboise, Calixte Lafontaine, and Isidore Dumas. We left most of the goods in the stores and guarded them.

Duck Lake

Nolin the traitor fled with the wife of his good brother Attanase Lepine. Many years later I met Nolin again and he said, "I am still your best friend. If I had to save myself it was because I was too scared." He also did not want us to get any of the good rifles from St. Laurent. He mentioned that I had been fair to everbody. In 1903 Nolin told me he would be my best friend until he died. During

Glenbow Archives, Calgary (photo no. NA 1063-1)

Gabriel Dumont at Fort Assiniboine, 1885

Batoche Nolin's wife and family stayed with Father Moulin.

◆ ◆ ◆

I am 65, and I was 47 during the rebellion. I am the son of Isidore Dumont. I was born in Winnipeg. We left there when I was very young and went to the Fort Pitt area where we stayed until I was 10. Then I returned to Winnipeg with my parents. I fired my first shot in a battle with the Sioux when I was 12.

During the 1870 rebellion I was camped at Batoche. Before leaving Winnipeg I told Riel, "if it comes to war send for me and I will come with the Indians."

Episodes of my Life

Once I killed a Blackfoot when I was fighting for the Cree. This Blackfoot was more daring than the rest: he came toward us all alone. I rode down on him. I had a good runner and managed to turn him, but he got away — so I chased him just like a buffalo, going from side to side. When I caught up to him I stuck the barrel of my rifle in his reins and fired. He fell forward onto the neck of my horse. At full gallop the surprise made him rear violently and almost threw me off backwards. The Blackfoot pony stayed right beside me. I passed my leg over the neck of my horse and jumped to the ground catching the riderless pony's bridle. Then I returned to check the Blackfoot. He was dead, and that caused me some pain because he had never done anything to me.

But you want to know why I killed him? This is why. Six or seven Métis tents were camped near a Cree camp.

We were on good terms with them. One day when I was not there, a Cree came to my tent and took a good horse I had left chained and locked. He wanted my horse to fight the Black-foot who were in the area, so he demanded the horse from my wife. She said no. So the Cree said, "if you don't open the lock I will kill the horse."

My wife did as he told her. When I got back and found this out I was very angry. That same night the Cree were having a war dance. I went into the lodge and stood among the women and didn't say anything. When they finished dancing I jumped up and joined the warriors and asked to speak.

"Friends, I have done this and I have done that. I will fight beside you here and now to show my courage. Then when I finish the enemy and they fear me, everyone will say that I am the best with a horse and rifle. But today you have done something to offend me. When I wasn't even there, you took my horse. It was not brave to scare my wife. Since I married her we have always been together, and what is done to my wife is done to me. I have told you what has happened. I will not let it pass."

The Cree said that this was not done to offend me, but that it was their law. Friends and allies were obliged to supply their best horses when they went to war.

"I do not follow your law," I said. "If you want me to go to war with you, there will be no one in front of me when we ride against the enemy. If it was any other way you could come and take my horse. But as long as I am always first to go up against the enemy, then nobody should touch my horses when I am not there."

The next day the Cree fought the Blackfoot and I went to battle with them. That is what led me to chase down the Blackfoot and kill him. I had to show the Cree that I was the best and that they should respect me.

◆ ◆ ◆

One day I was out scouting for Buffalo. I left my horse tied foot to halter and climbed a butte. I was not quite at the top when I saw something hiding across from me on the other side among some rocks. I slid down face first and worked my way behind the hill. It was either a man or a wolf stretched out on its side. If I yelled, a man would listen, a wolf would run. I watched for a while then cried out. It was a man. He did not move but seemed to listen for a long time. I thought he must be asleep, but I had to see this for myself. I went back down, took my horse, went around the base of the two hills, and went to the top of the one where the man slept. If I tried to get close to him he might have gotten the jump on me. So I got off my horse and left him. When I got closer I saw the man asleep, with his rifle on the ground beside him. I had my rifle in hand, ready to fire. If I woke him he would be scared, and he would go for his gun and shoot me. So I moved closer, quietly, like a wolf, almost right up to him, and took his rifle away slowly and quietly. Then I fell back and put the gun on the ground behind me. Now there would be no danger, so I went ahead and woke him up. I kept up my guard as I talked with him — after all he might be an enemy. He had a full head of matted hair and a large strong body. He was a Gros Ventre. Soon he was on his knees in front of me, his face begging for mercy. I started to laugh and he soon saw that I was not going to hurt him. I sat beside him, keeping my rifle on the other side, took out my pipe and lit it. The Indian took it gladly and smoked deeply. Then his whole body began to shake and he could not hold the pipe. He showed me by signs that that was how much I had scared him. Finally we got up and I led him to his rifle. Then we moved to my horse which was hobbled. I realized I would have to bend over to untie the legs but I was afraid to try, afraid he would shoot me as I bent over. So I signed to the Gros Ventre that he should go and get his own horse at the bottom of the hill. He did. And to the pain of his horse he left at top speed like the devil was after him. I left soon after.

◆ ◆ ◆

Another time, when I was young, I saw a Blood man on the prairie. We rode at each other never doubting the other would turn his bridle first. When I got near I recognized his tribe and he turned away. He was armed, but our meeting had been so quick and unexpected, he did not have time to draw an arrow from his quiver. Seeing this, I did not want to hurt him, just unsaddle him. Now our horses were shoulder to shoulder. The Blood would not stop his horse. I was right beside him so I pulled up on my reins and jumped up behind him. I grabbed both his arms so he could not defend himself. I took him back to camp that way, and gave him a pipe. He smoked it without getting off his horse. Then I told him he could go and he left as fast as the horse could carry him.

A long time later when I was making peace between our nations I met one of my old prisoners in one of their camps. It was twenty years later, and even though the Gros Ventre now had white hair among his black locks I recognized him. He was Bull Hide, a grand chief of his nation.

◆ ◆ ◆

I was going to make peace in a Sioux camp, and just as I was leaving the tent where I was staying, bending down through the narrow opening that was closed by a hanging skin, a Sioux hit me over the head with his rifle as he pulled the trigger. I was lucky the shot missed but I was left with a bruise. The other Sioux kicked and beat him with sticks. He had dishonoured them and was driven from camp.

In 1891 when I was in the United States, I was almost assassinated. I was camped near some other Métis, alone in my tent. During the night I was awakened by a knife blow behind my left ear. I jumped up, throwing off my attacker. I had done him no harm, so why did he want to hurt me? I asked what he was trying to do. "What do you want?" I asked a few times, I wasn't even angry — just surprised to have a man I had never seen before trying to kill me. He was Herculean, armed like a butcher ready to carve.

The assassin stabbed me many times in the back. Finally I managed to pin him with my knees on his shoulders. I grabbed his hands. During the struggle the killer had slashed my stomach twice, once on the left side just below the ribs, and once a bit lower, under the navel. Each wound was about four or five inches long and left big scars.

The wounds had a horribly enticing beauty and made a great show on my stomach. I held my assassin in great respect. My right hand was halfway down his throat, and he was gagging. I grabbed the knife with my left hand, cutting the fingers to the bone. The nearby tents woke to the noise. When they saw me almost choking my enemy they pulled me off him and let him go. He fled. I think it was somebody after the $5000.00 prize the government had put on my head.

My wound at the Battle of Duck Lake

I suffered through the whole war, from Fish Creek to Batoche, shouting all day long. My head bled all night. When I arrived in the States, the wound started to bleed again. I tried to fix it myself. There was a cut two inches long and three-quarters of an inch deep, right on the top of my head. It was lucky I had a very thick skull or I would have been killed. The doctors told me a main artery had been cut. I had many accidents right after the war. When I coughed hard it was like being hit over the head with a hammer, and many times I lost consciousness and fell. But most of the time I would fall and recover right away. One day in a blacksmith's shop I fell face first on top of a pile of angle iron and marked up my whole face. Since then the accidents haven't happened much. The circulation has no doubt been restored by the nearby arteries growing little by little to replace the cut one.

◆ ◆ ◆

I was supposed to have been in France with Buffalo Bill. It is not true! I worked for Buffalo Bill, but only in America, and that was before 1889. During his trip to Europe, Buffalo Bill was going to pass through England and I did not have my amnesty so I could not go.

With Buffalo Bill in France were Michel Dumas, Ambroise Lepine — brother of old Maxime Lepine, general in the 1870 rebellion, but no part of the "rebellion" of 1885 — Jules Marion, son of Edouard Marion, and Maxime Goulet, brother of Roger Goulet — lately the head of the land bureau in Winnipeg. Michel Dumas and Ambroise Lepine did not stay long with Buffalo Bill. They were almost always drunk and were shown the door. Lepine pretended that he had been mistaken for Buffalo Bill and that it was jealousy that got him fired. They were out on the streets, so they went to knock on the door of the Canadian consul in Paris. That is when Dumas tried to pass for me. M. Pierre Fourrin, a secretary at the Canadian consulate, was asked to present them to the mayor of the Commune of Neuilly where Buffalo Bill's show was set up.

"General," said Fourrin, "I wish to present to you Generals Dumont and Lepine of the Army of the Métis Rebellion in Canada."

The General took an interest in them as he would show good will to any brother-in-arms. It was because of his intervention with the Canadian consul that Michel Dumas returned to Canada as me, Gabriel Dumont.

Ambroise Lepine was brought back by the son of Adolphe Ouimet, a Montreal lawyer. Goulet was also shown the door by Buffalo Bill. His brother sent him the money to come home. Jules Marion, who was hired to drive a dog team, stayed his full time.

I went to France once in 1895 for one year and never left Paris. I got my amnesty in the winter of 1886, one year after the others.

My Story

Around 1880 or 1881, the Métis of Batoche and St. Laurent got very tired of having to pay for wood they cut for planks and firewood. I led the discontent. I could not understand why this was happening, since it was still wild country. In Manitoba, four or five years after it became a province we could still cut wood on unoccupied land for free. Father Vegreville, who was against this as well, and I drew up a petition together.

One day I went to find Laforte, (Louis Smitte) and told him we could not take this any more. He told me, "you cannot stop it: the law is passed."

I answered him, "I will try everything."

We called a meeting at Batoche. They wanted me to be president but I said no, because I wanted to do more than talk. So they made Emmanuel Champagne president. I told them again how the government had become the master of our country. "We left Manitoba because we were not free, and we came to this new wild country to be free. And now we have to pay to cut firewood? Where can we go? What can we do? We cannot let this happen. The government has made its first move against us and if we let them get away with it, there will be more laws coming."

The meeting decided to make another petition. Michel Dumas, also known as the Rat, closed his office. He was the agent in charge of siezing the wood. He offered to sign the petition, and at the same time keep right on siezing the wood until a new order came about.

I said to him, "we have no need of your signature. You are exactly who we don't need. We are working against you."

"Oh Mister Dumont," said Dumas, "I want to sign to show my sympathy for the rest of you."

I kept the petition in my hand until my Uncle Isidore took it, and I told him, "Listen to what Gabriel says: he does not want you to sign, understand?"

Then I went to find Clarke, who lived at Fort Carlton and was the district representative in the assembly. (Batoche and Alex Cayen were our other two representatives.) When we arrived at Carlton, we told Clarke the reason for our visit. "We have been forced to pay for wood we cut here in the wilderness. We cannot let that happen. This tax is too much. We have come to you to find a way to stop this, because you are our representative. You must see that this is not right — and if you do not do something about it there will be more to come." Clarke answered that he could do nothing himself: the law had been passed. All the representatives were there when it was, and they were all in favour of it.

"Well," I said "if it has become a law it must be abolished. I will make you — I will force you — to make the trip. If you won't go, then we do not need a representative."

"No, there is nothing I can do," answered Clarke. "It isn't even worth trying."

"Try it!" Here is a paper." I took the petition from my pocket." Take it with you to Winnipeg. And get going — there is not much time."

Clarke looked at the petition with all the signatures and said, "with this, of course I'll go. But you didn't tell me what you had done, Mister Dumont. I will get to work on this with pleasure because with this I can get you some service, some relief from the chambers where I am the member for this district. I am going to telegraph right away and if they don't answer me I will go to Winnipeg — at government expense, of course." In five days he got the answer: an order allowing the Métis of the Saskatchewan to cut wood freely for their own use.

Michel Dumas got the news of this new measure and a few days later met Jean Dumont, whose wood he had siezed before, and told him he could have it back. Jean who was cutting wood told him, "it is a good day today, I can cut all I can carry. There was never any doubt when we went to work against you."

This all happened around 1881 or 1882. Around this same time we also saw that the Métis of Edmonton were being pushed off their land by new settlers. When they reported this to the police they were told that nothing could be done. The Métis were the first to live there, and claimed squatters' rights. There were about thirty Métis families who had been forced out, and they decided to get justice for themselves. They accused the government of ignoring their rights to the land which had been signed over to these new occupants, whom the government represented. They threatened to pull the small houses of the settlement down with their horses and some ropes. The settlers naturally became very irritated. But the Métis did not leave soon, and came very close to spilling blood.

The Métis of the Saskatchewan learned of their fate and feared that the same might happen to them. The problems we were having with the government and the wood superintendent were not good signs. We did not want to have to fight for our rights which had been won in the rebellion of 1870. But we were resolved to demand our rights from the government.

During 1882 or 1883 we were greatly occupied with this issue. We had meetings that were my idea, along with Charles Nolin and others, at Batoche, St. Laurent, and just this side of Prince Albert. We petitioned the government but never got an answer. The last meeting in this period was held at the home of my father, Isidore Dumont. He had become discouraged, and only wanted to know how we could quickly and easily obtain our rights. An English Métis named Andrew Spence answered, "there is only one man who can help us now: Riel."

Everyone agreed. Riel was the only one who could intervene between the Métis and the government in 1870, and that negotiation had made those rights a reality. It was quickly decided to bring Riel back to the Saskatchewan to help us draw up petitions, and use his contacts and abilities. We wanted a treaty like the one he had negotiated with the government. (Riel's papers were found by Baptiste Rochelot after the battle. He left them

Glenbow Archives, Calgary (photo no. NA 1177-1)

with a priest from Winnipeg named Campo, who was originally from Montreal and had come to Batoche with Lemieux after the rebellion.)

Jimmie Isbister and I were asked to go and find Riel. The people would look after our families while we were gone. Moise Ouellette and Michel Dumas volunteered to go with us because they wanted to meet Riel and would beg him in case he did not want to come back. Lafontaine and Gardupuy were going to Lewiston to look for Lafontaine's mother. They came with us part of the way. I had a small simple wagon. Moise and Jimmie each had two hitch wagons.

It was my first trip to Montana, but somehow I knew exactly how long it would be to the Mission of Saint Pierre. So I said before I left, "the fifteenth day after we leave here, you will know we are getting close."

In fact, we left on the nineteenth of May and on the morning of June fourth we arrived. Riel was teaching there with the Fathers. It was exactly 8 o'clock when we entered the courtyard of the Mission. Mass had just begun. We waited in a small house that Jimmie Swan lived in. We asked him where Riel was and he told us that Riel was helping with mass, as he did every day. I then spoke to an old woman named Arcand who said she would go and speak to Riel right away, and let him know that there were some people who wished to speak to him right away.

Riel left the chapel and came toward Swan's house. When I saw him I went out to meet him with my hand outstretched. Riel took my hand and held it in his and said to me, "you are a man who has travelled far. I don't know you, but you seem to know me."

"Yes," I answered, "and I think you might know the name Gabriel Dumont."

"Of course, quite well," answered Riel, "I know it well. It is good to see you but, if you will excuse me, I am going to hear the rest of the mass. Please go and wait for me at my home, over there, the house near the small bridge. My wife is there and I will be there shortly."

After returning from mass, Riel asked why we from the Northwest had come to see him and what we wanted. He seemed surprised and flattered by what he heard. As he answered us I knew that I would always remember his words: "God has helped me understand why you have made this long trip, and since there are four of you who have arrived on the fourth, and you wish to leave with a fifth, I cannot answer today. You must wait until the fifth. I will give you my answer in the morning." We were not in too great a hurry — we could wait one day before leaving. So we would wait until the morning for an answer. The next day, as he promised, Riel gave his answer: "It has been fifteen years since I gave my heart to my country. I am ready to give it again now, but I cannot leave my little family. If you can arrange for them to come I will go with you."

"Good," we answered. "With our three wagons we can make room."

Riel had his wife, a son about four years old, and a two-year-old daughter. "But," added Riel," I cannot leave for eight days. I am employed as a teacher here and I would like to make arrangements to leave properly." We waited, as he asked, during this delay, and on the eighth day we started our trip.

After a few days we arrived at Belton, Montana. Riel took mass and afterward he went to the priest to ask for his blessing. The priest told him that he didn't see why he should give his blessing. Nevertheless, since we were stopping for twenty-four hours to rest the horses, the next morning, Riel went to mass again. After mass the priest came to find him and told him, "yesterday I answered you as I did because I didn't think my blessing would be useful. But since I see you still want it, I will give it to you."

Riel accepted and left to find us because he wanted all of us to receive the priest's blessing. I was the only one who wanted to go to the church for this. Riel also brought his wife and children. All five of us kneeled at the communion table to receive the blessing Riel had asked for. Immedi-ately after we left and were back on the trail, I made up a commemorative prayer for this blessing. It just came out of my mouth: "Father, give me courage, and my belief and my faith in the holy blessing I have received in Your holy name, in order that I will remember it all of my life right up to the hour of my death. Amen."

The twenty-second day after we left the mission of St. Pierre we arrived at Fish Creek, where sixty Métis had come to meet us. That night we camped at my place, some in the house, the rest nearby in tents. It was the fifth of July, 1884. The next day we left for Batoche. I went ahead to get Father Moulin to prepare the church where Riel was to make a speech. But so many wanted to hear him, when he got there he realized that the church was too small. So he spoke to the crowd which had followed him, outside behind the church. He spoke of rights, treaties and other matters.

Riel stayed first at Moise Ouellette's. Then he went to Charles Nolin's with his family and stayed there until the rebellion. (I don't know whether Riel ever bought the Prince Albert Journal, as Caron reported.) The summer and winter passed, and during this time many meetings and petitions were made. One of the last meetings was held at Joseph Arcroix's in February, 1885. None of the old petitions, all addressed to the government in Ottawa, were ever answered. In the end, Riel and the other leaders of the movement were losing patience, and one day he let the words slip: "they should at least answer us, either yes or no. And they cannot say no, since we are only asking for what has already been promised. If they don't give us our rights we will have to rebel again."

After that the word rebellion was on the tongue of every Métis, along with the tragic meaning it had already acquired. We all remembered the rebellion of 1870 which had been very passive and there had been only one victim. Scott got what he deserved for his extreme fanaticism. This time the Métis who were talking about rebellion felt that a noisy threat would bring them their rights. These were the memories that were held in everyone's minds. No people in the world are as strong and good as the Métis. Given a choice between riches and their rights, they would choose their rights and everything would be right in the end.

But then there was still Clarke, the representative of the townspeople of Fort Carlton, who had returned from Winnipeg by way of Qu'Appelle. When he passed through Batoche he asked those who were there, "have you had more meetings? What have you been doing all this time? Did you get your answer?'

Then Clarke told them, "Good, good — it won't be long now. There are eighty soldiers coming. I saw them at Humboldt, and tomorrow or the next day Riel and Dumont will be taken."

Naturally everyone was excited. The next afternoon we had a general meeting at the church. Riel and I addressed the crowd. I told the crowd the latest news: "The police are coming to take Riel." I also asked the people, "what are you going to do? Here is a man who has done so much for us. Are we going to let him slide through our hands? Let us make a plan."

Riel then spoke: "We send petitions, they send police to take us — Gabriel Dumont and me. But I know very well how this works. It is I who have done wrong. The government hates me because I have already made them give in once. This time they will give up nothing. I also think it would be better for me to go now. I must leave you and I feel I should go now. Once I am gone you may be able to get what you want more easily. Yes — I really think that it would be better if I went back to Montana."

The whole crowd interrupted and told him "no, we won't let you go. You have worked hard for our rights and you can't quit now."

"Then," said Riel, "if I must I will desert."

"If you desert, we will desert with you."

I answered them: "It is for the best that we go and cross the line. We will not be insulted and made prisoners."

"We won't let that happen. Don't be afraid of that," answered the crowd.

"So what will you do?"

"When they come, we will take up arms and no one will lay a hand on you!"

"What are you saying?" I asked. "You talk of taking up arms. But what arms do you have to battle the government? And how many of you are there?"

"Yes!" They answered as one. "We will take up arms if you want us to."

Riel would not say whether he would stay. So I continued: "'Yes,' you say. I know you well, I know all of you like my children. I know how much you are all for taking up arms. It is good to be firm, but not everyone is. So I ask again, how many will take up arms? All in favour of taking up arms raise your hands."

Instead of only raising one hand, the whole crowd rose as one. There were cries of joy and they yelled, "if we are to die for our country, we will die together."

I was frozen. Even though I was the most enthusiastic one there and capable of any heroism in the face of danger, I tried to remain calm and take judgment into account. I said again, "I can see that you have made your decision, but I wonder if you will become tired and discouraged. Me — I will never give up, but how many will be there with me? Two or three?"

"We will all be with you, right to the end!" answered the whole crowd.

"Good then," I said. "This is good, if you really want to take up arms, I will lead you as I always have."

"Good then. If you will lead us, that is good — to arms, to arms."

It was done. The armed rebellion had begun. Without the news that Clarke had reported — that the police were coming to take Riel — no one ever dreamed that a military insurgence would come again. Now it was here. In any case, we had tried all peaceful means to obtain our rights. It was Clarke who put fire to the powder by reporting the news. The news was false. It was invented to scare off the organizers of the meetings.

Thirty men went to search for arms and then returned. After we had decided to take up arms, we left the church and went toward Norbert Delorme's house. (Now Laderonte's.) The crowd stayed there with me while Riel and Napoleon Nault toured up to the edge of Fish Creek.

Then I said, "now when I see a government man, I will take him prisoner. You may think I am going too far, but no. The moment we took up arms, we were in rebellion, and this is not too much."

Right at that moment the Indian agent arrived with his man, coming from the reserve.

"I am taking you prisoner," I told him.

"Oh. Why?"

"We have taken up arms against the government and we are going to take all those who work for the government prisoners."

"That's good," said the agent. "Take us."

Sometime after we heard a cart coming up the trail. I saw Jardine and went down the path to arrest him. He whipped his horse.

"Stop!" I yelled.

Jardine pushed his horse.

"Stop!" I yelled again.

Jardine whipped his horse again.

"If you don't stop I will shoot your horse!" I yelled, putting my hand on my rifle. This time Jardine stopped.

"Where are you going?" I asked.

"It's none of your business where I'm going."

"There will be no problem if you tell the truth about your trip, but this is no honest trip. You are going to Duck Lake to report what has happened, and I am making you prisoner."

"But my horse, and the one I am leading?"

"Your horse is also a prisoner."

"But I am looking for medicine for my wife who is sick. I am trying to take it to her."

"Give it to me," I said. "I will get it to her."

I took the medicine and Jardine stayed prisoner. While this was happening Riel returned and wanted to know what had happened since he had left. I told him we had already taken three prisoners.

"Yes! Yes that's good," said Riel.

Then we headed back towards the church and stopped at Jarreau's house where we stayed awhile. That evening, the eighteenth of March, we raided Baker's store. That same evening we also arrested two men who were trying to repair the telegraph. They were taken by captains Isidore Dumont, Augustin Laframboise, and their men. I stayed at Batoche. When they crossed the river with their two prisoners, I went out to meet them.

"Have you disarmed them?" I asked. And when they answered no I said, "oh well, you have done your duty as captains."
So I searched them myself, but they didn't have any guns.

The Peace Mission of Mitchell and Tom MacKay

Mitchell and Tom MacKay came to Jarreau's house to try and calm our spirits. Tom MacKay accused Riel of being the cause of all the trouble. "As for Gabriel," he said, "I think he doesn't understand what is happening. He has made a mistake."

I answered "Tom, you may be mistaken. I have not been told what to do. When someone tells me something, I understand. I am not mistaken, like you. You have gone against us, and still you are a Métis and have the same rights to gain as we do. I don't know if you have even a small spoonful of good sense. Your blood is all water. If it wasn't for our friendship, I would take you prisoner."

Mitchell had no answer.

It was finally decided that Riel would send two men to accompany these two back to the police coming from Carlton in order to deliver a message. The two men sent by Riel were Nolin and Max Lepine. They went with them to the police, but the papers were never delivered and we never found out why.

The Pillage of Mitchell's store, March 24

It was reported that Mitchell had said, "if they want to come and take my guns, I will fight them with a pitchfork."

At this time I told Riel, "you have given them all the advantages. They are coming to Duck Lake: we could catch them crossing the lake. And while we're there, why don't we take Mitchell's store? We have taken up arms and we just sit here. If we wanted to move now we could catch them by surprise."

"But," said Riel, "it won't be easy. They won't just let us get away with it."

"Give me ten men and put me in charge."

Riel agreed, and I chose ten men and set out. I chose from the committed: Edouard Dumont, Phillippe Gardupuy, Baptiste Deschamps, Baptiste Arcand, Baptiste Ouellette, Norbert Delorme, Joseph Delorme, and Augustin Laframboise.

We left Batoche an hour after noon. Mitchell knew we were coming, so when we arrived the store was closed. An English Métis named Magnus Burstein, a farmer from Duck Lake, was found nearby. He was also a clerk in the store, and he told me it was locked.

"Fine, fine," I said. "We'll break down the doors." And I went to do it.

"Well," said Burstein, "they left me the keys: here they are."

We went in the store but all the guns had disappeared. We did find some lead shot in the latrine ditch. We stayed a moment, and then we were told somebody was coming. Soon after Riel arrived with all the men from Batoche. When they got there I sent my ten men to go and watch the Carlton Trail — I didn't trust that the police wouldn't try a surprise attack. We crossed Duck Lake on the ice, stopped at the reserve, and looked after our horses until nightfall. Then I chose two of my men, Baptiste Arcand and Baptiste Ouellette, to go and watch the road. Before long they returned to say they had seen two policemen.

I took my brother Edouard, Baptiste Deschamps, Phillippe Gardupuy, and an Indian who wanted to go along, and left the others at the reserve. We went to find the two policemen who had been spotted. I took a Canadian government grey. "If they try to defend themselves," I said, "we will kill them. If not, we will not harm them." We left at a gallop by the light of the moon.

We talked under our breath as we returned to the exact spot where they had seen the police. Then on the big bluff at the edge of the woods, we saw the two policemen riding side by side. We moved toward them under cover. When we got to the top of the bluff we were at a good distance to start our charge, and I yelled, "go — turn your horses loose! Get them!"

There was a hard crust on the snow and it was impossible to go off the path. I had the best horse and was trying to catch up to the horsemen, but decided to wait for the rest to reach the top of the hill, to give the horses good footing. When all the horses had arrived we were still right behind the policemen, as I had hoped. I was still mounted and came up on the left side of the two and said to them, "stop! If you try to escape I will kill you."

"Why?" asked the rider. "I am a surveyor."

"What are you trying to tell me?" I answered. "There is nothing to survey out here at this time of night." At the same time I passed my leg across the neck of my horse and grabbed the policeman by the arms, pulled him off his horse, and fell to the ground with him. Phillippe Gardupuy and Baptiste Deschamps went after the other policeman. Because I had made my move first, the road was blocked and they couldn't catch up to him right away. So Baptiste Deschamps yelled, "stop or I'll kill you!"

There can be no doubt the policeman heard him and understood. He turned around to look back, and right then the movement of his hands changed the footing of his horse. The horse suddenly stumbled, and the policeman fell off. Phillippe Gardupuy passed on my right and went to arrest him. Baptiste Deschamps was already on top of him and without stopping completely, jumped to the ground and siezed the policeman by the arms. Gardupuy arrived at the same time to help. I had disarmed my prisoner and went to disarm the other one saying, "you are my prisoners, and I am taking you to Duck Lake." The policemen asked for their horses. "You can use these others, but we will not give you your own back." I chose the worst and gave them each one, but the policemen preferred to walk.

When we arrived back at Mitchell's store, the policemen asked for sheriff Ross. "He isn't sheriff tonight," I laughed. "I have taken him prisoner. He is under guard with the other prisoners at Batoche."

We went right back out to watch the Carlton Trail. We went to the same spot but saw nothing more. When day came we thought the police wouldn't risk sending any more scouts, so we retired. We got back to Duck Lake and had just put our horses in the stable, when we heard the cry: "Here come the police!"

In fact it was three policemen who were scouting up to Duck Lake. Quickly we found horses to go after them, and some had already left before I got my horse saddled. I wanted to be at the front so I strained to catch them, but instead of following the path, I picked my way over the snow. I trusted my horse, but we got caught in deep drifts and lost more time. I was a quarter mile behind Jim Short and Patrice Fleury. As they chased them, the three policemen were joined by Tom MacKay who told them "quickly — save yourselves! Because Gabriel is going to take this whole unit prisoner, just like the other two."

Edouard Dumont had joined Fleury and Short in chasing the three Mounted Police almost back to the troop. There were twenty sleighs. One had been stopped and turned sideways to prepare a defense against our attack. As they approached, a policeman yelled from one of the sleighs "stop or we'll kill you!"

They stopped but stayed on their horses. When I arrived behind them I said to them "what are you doing? Why are you still on your horses? You can see they are going to kill you. Get off your horses and get ready to defend yourselves."

I got off my horse and chased it away with a slap on the neck. I took my carbine and advanced toward the police to harass them. When we were about twenty-five yards away, a sergeant in the second sleigh yelled "if you don't stop, I will kill you!"

Just then he saw me with my carbine. "Don't try it," I yelled at him. "I will kill you first." I shouldered my gun and aimed it at the sergeant. He put his rifle across his knees, and I moved up so I was about fifteen yards away. In two or three jumps, I was at the sleigh and on top of the sergeant who had time to lift his rifle. I hit him in the chest with the barrel of my rifle, and he fell back in the sleigh, his rifle pointed straight up in the air. Because he had gloves on, it went off by mistake. The sergeant got back up in the sleigh and threatened me with his rifle.

"Don't even move, or I will kill you."

Tom MacKay, on horseback a short distance away, yelled to me "look out: if you don't stop, it'll be the end for you."

I answered him "You watch out. This is all your fault, all of it. You brought the police and whatever happens will be your responsibility. Don't you realize there are Canadian Métis fighting to the death with us?"

As MacKay answered, I lifted my rifle to take a swing at him. He tried to turn his horse, but this put his hind legs off the path, on the high side, and he sank deeply in the snow. The rider was now lower and I had a better chance to hit him. I swung, but the horse made a quick movement and stopped at an opening in the trail. The end of the rifle slid over MacKay's back. He spurred his horse, and shot forward. I took another swing, but only got the horse on the buttocks.

A policeman in another sleigh took aim at me and was going to kill me. But when I took aim, he put his gun across his knees. At the same time all the sleighs started. Jim Short and Patrice Fleury stayed on horseback at a distance. Only Edouard Dumont, at my urging, had gotten off his horse and advanced toward them while I was talking this warlike way. As the sleighs were starting to move, Edouard ran to the first and tried to climb on by grabbing the harness. He wanted to take the whole convoy prisoner. They pushed him back and he tumbled into the snow. All the sleighs left at a gallop in the direction of Carlton.

Jim Short was yelling insults after them, but I said to him "what are you trying to do! You didn't even get off your horse and now that they are gone you fire off your silliness. If that is all you are going to do, you will be well-rested and your feet will stay warm."

We returned to Duck Lake, and the others who arrived at the end turned back as well. We put our horses in the stable again and sat down to lunch. We had just finished when we heard the police were coming again. We all left to go and waited at the big hill just off the side.

We met a party of scouts, and followed them. They made it back to the main troop. While we were going after them I told my brother, Isidore, "I don't want to start killing them, I want to take prisoners. If they try to kill us then we will kill them."

When we got to the police I saw that all the sleighs were off the path. There was no pattern, but they were well-placed for battle. Not far off the trail there was a small, low foundation. I didn't even slow down, but left the trail and was soon at the wall with my men. Twenty-five jumped from their horses and went on the defensive.

Crozier himself came forward. Isidore Dumont and an Indian went out to meet him. Crozier and the Indian, who was unarmed, put out their hands. Then a policeman and an English Métis named McKay moved his horse forward a step, and the Indian jumped him and tried to take his rifle. It didn't work.

Most thought that the Indian who was killed by the policeman was the first victim of the war. But I think it might have been Isidore who was killed first. The Indian was unarmed and my brother had his rifle, and the policeman had to kill the armed man first so he would not be killed by him. Even if the policeman had killed the Indian first, I had no doubt that my brother had been killed right after. He was killed without firing his gun — we found it by his side. Edouard Dumont said that after the first shot he saw the Indian still standing, trying to return. And although he hadn't seen the exact moment he had fallen, he was not the victim of the first shot. This Indian was the godson of Charles Trottier. He did not die quickly, not until we arrived at Duck Lake.

After the first shot I ordered my men to get up and fire. This fight lasted twenty minutes. Riel was in the small hollow with us. He was on his horse, a crucifix in his hand, held up in the air. He would not get down from his horse. He was very exposed — the small hollow was not deep enough for a mounted man to be in cover. Riel, Isidore, the Indian, and I were on horseback. I had thought that Isidore had been killed on his horse, but now I doubt it. The Indian was killed while on foot, since he had left his little pony behind. I was in the hole fifty or sixty yards from the Indian and Isidore. We knew that the police were from Carlton, but we had no idea they were going to attack. Riel had come to Duck Lake because he was afraid to stay at Batoche alone.

We heard about the fire at Fort Carlton the next morning. Jackson's brother was staying at Duck Lake, with our permission, to visit his brother. He was helping to care for the wounded, as were the police we had made prisoners at Duck Lake. Hilaire Paternotre had wintered near Fort Carlton, and stayed for a while after the battle. He put out the fire at the Fort.

As we began to turn the enemy, one of them gave the signal to depart. I was hidden behind a small bluff, and I saw a sleigh cross an opening in the trees. I told my men I would give them trouble when they tried to climb in the sleigh. When a policeman showed his face a bullet in the head made him fall back in the sleigh. Then I yelled to my men: "Courage. Follow me. I am going to board the sleighs, hear me?" Just as I came upon the enemy who were firing right at me, I fell, seated on the snow. A bullet creased the top of my head making a furrow, and the ricochet whistled away. Blood spurted into the air. Delorme yelled to me "oh no — they got you!"

But I answered him, "when you don't lose your head, you're not dead." At the same time I told Baptiste Vandal, "cousin take my rifle!" Vandal left his old rifle there and took my fourteen shot re-peater. "Good — take my cartridges too." Vandal unhooked my belt, "No not that one," I said. "Undo the other one." I then tried to get up to my knees, but it was my gun belt that held up my pants. Vandal didn't do it up and my pants fell down.

My brother Edouard had been hit over by the edge of a small ravine, and he slid and pulled himself over to me and cover. Augustin Laframboise was stretched out near-by. He had dragged himself there and tried to get to his knees to make the sign, but he fell again on his side. I said to him, "do not be afraid. Soon you will be all right." But Laframboise was already dead: a bullet had passed through his chest.

By then the English were completely in flight. Edouard Dumont shouted, "after them! Exterminate them!" But Riel, always with his crucifix in hand, said, "we have had enough of that. Let them go."

They put me on my horse and tied my head with handkerchiefs. When I passed my brother Isidore, I got down but I couldn't tell if he was dead. A little further on I was told, "behind that bluff there is a young volunteer, wounded in the leg." I went around the fence and came up to him: I was going to finish him off. I told him it would be quick and painless. I reached for my revolver, but it was right in the middle of my back and I couldn't reach it from the left or the right. While I was trying to get my gun, Riel arrived and stopped me from killing him.

You may ask why I wanted to kill the wounded. They came to fight against us and I was shocked at the way my brother was killed and that they had shaved me. We cared for their wounded with ours.

We returned to Duck Lake before noon. Riel gave a speech at once. The world rained blood, he said. "You deserve congratulations as does your leader Mister Dumont. Let us give him three cheers." They saluted me with cheers.

The English had left many of their dead on the field, so Riel told them they could come and recover them. He sent an envoy, a prisoner taken at Humboldt, with a letter from Riel and me, giving our promise that there was no risk.

We gave the prisoner a disguise and a horse to take him to Carlton. He delivered the letter, but the English thought it was a trap. Better yet — they accused the prisoner of being an accomplice in the ambush and made him a prisoner in the fort.

I wanted to attack, and stop the police. But Riel was against that, saying it was too savage to go and attack them at night. I was very upset by Riel's opposition, and told him, "if you are going to give them the advantage like that, we cannot win."

The Métis who were near the fire at Fort Carlton saved part of the spoils. St. Denis told me, "if you want to come to the Pines, we can destroy them." But I was very tired. I had to sleep on the march: it was my second night without sleep. When the police got back to Prince Albert, the prisoner who had taken the letter from Riel protested his innocence again. This time they believed him and set him free.

The day after the fighting, the bodies were still laying in the sun. Riel sent two sleighs, and the men carried the bodies into one of the two small houses near the battlefield. The next day three sleighs arrived from Prince Albert to take the dead. Jackson, the brother of Riel's secretary, remained with the prisoners. The police came almost to Duck Lake, where they unharnessed and cared for their horses. There were nine dead bodies. Jackson's brother stayed with us: the secretary had already gone mad. The total number of Métis fighters was about 200, including Indians, but they weren't all armed, especially the Indians. Many had not much more than sticks. There was one who was armed with a staff, with a curved top, used to dig potatoes. The Sioux of Saskatoon or Round Prairie, had not come yet. Some came before Fish Creek, and the rest came before Batoche. In that little valley and the two houses, there had been about twenty-five fighters.

They didn't fire much, but they took an effective part in a short fight.

It was during the battle of Duck Lake that Nolin ran away. He hadn't gone over to the enemy when the cry "here come the police!" came. When he heard the rifle shots he went wild with terror. He took a small white pony belonging to Belanger's son and ran just like we knew he would, just like a fox. He had been in at the beginning of the rebellion and had always been one with the Métis. He made this tragic choice because he was afraid for his safety, and began to question our plans. I decided to execute him. It happened sometime between the declaration of the rebellion and Duck Lake. I sent three men to find him, but he had fled to the priest's house at St. Laurent Mission.

We returned to Batoche the following day and called a meeting at G. Fisher's house. I was staying at Batoche's house. Only his mother and children were there. His son-in-law Eugene Boucher, a store clerk who later became a deputy, Batoche's brother Isidore, Baptiste Boyer, and Fisher were gone.

It was also then that we brought all the families to Batoche. We fed all the animals that the Sioux and Métis had rounded up, from near the English Métis settlements. Some had made common cause with us from the start but had since stopped marching with us, so we treated them as enemies. We treated the animals taken in the rebellion exactly the same way.

Fish Creek

At the news of Middleton's arrival, Riel wanted to stay and defend Batoche, but my plan was to go out and meet the enemy, because they were already showing weakness by hesitating to advance. Besides, we had nothing to lose. This time we followed my plan and on the twenty-third we left to meet Middleton. Riel and I had about 150 men with us. We left Edouard Dumont at Batoche to guard the prisoners. We followed the trail along the bank of the river, some on horses, others on foot. There were Métis, Sioux, and Cree. Riel kept making us stop so he could say the rosary.

About four miles out we came to the edge of the coulee at Roger Goulet's and we stopped to eat. It was midnight, and we killed and ate two animals. When we finished, Emmanuel Champagne and Moise Carriere arrived, sent by Edouard, who wanted the help of thirty men led by either Riel or me: a troop of police had been spotted on the trail from Qu'Appelle.

I refused to turn back, and even though Riel himself had not been asked, he offered. Most of the fighters had left Batoche with some regret, wanting to protect their families. Riel wanted to take fifty men. There would be blood everywhere, so I chose the men who would return, and stayed with one hundred.

We marched on. "This time," I said, "we won't be saying rosary so much, so we'll move faster." We were almost to McIntoche's, and it was almost daylight. The Sioux came to me and said they would not attack the government by day, and they would not be forced. They wanted to return.

My plan had been to surprise the enemy camp during the night, to spring a prairie fire on them, take advantage of their confusion, and massacre them. If we had found the English camp that first night, Middleton's soldiers would have been lucky to get out alive.

I decided to go back and wait for the enemy at Fish Creek coulee. Ignace Poitras, also known as Betillet, had a good runner and said to me, "take my horse and go find out where they are." One of the Touronds had a good horse and gave it to Napoleon Nault. We went together to scout the enemy. I ordered the men not to use the trail, to leave no signs for the enemy by staying on the prairie. They paid little attention to my orders, and when I returned they had made many fires right on the path.

Napoleon Nault and I got to within a half mile of the English camp. I thought we might meet a scout, and I was afraid that Nault might try and capture him. I wanted to get behind them, kill them, and take their guns. That was always my first thought: to get more guns. We scouted the prairie around their camp without seeing a single scout, so we returned to join the men at Fish Creek. It was a short day. Since it was their place, the Touronds gave us an animal.

I was constantly sending out scouts. Gabriel Bertrand brought the news that the enemy was near, just as we finished breakfast. It was the thirty scouts. I placed my men on the bluff and moved forward with twenty horsemen. I ordered my men to let the first of the enemy come all the way down to the creek and only then fire from above, when they were all strung out along the trail near the bluff. If any were left behind, my horsemen would cut them down and take their arms. But the advance guard of the enemy saw tracks on the trail and returned to the troop. The English finally found us when some of the scouts broke away. One of them advanced almost to our lines. "Let them come," I said, "and when enough of them get close we will get them."

But they would not come any closer, there wasn't even a good chance to fire a shot. I wanted to slaughter them and get their guns. A group of horsemen charged the scouts. Horses were everywhere and I was cut off again and again, but finally I caught up to the scouts. I was about fifteen yards away when I heard someone behind yell, "there they are — the police." I got off two shots, but none fell. They got to a small bluff and took cover there. Meanwhile, I noticed the English soldiers moving through the trees. I stopped my horse and turned around in the middle of the nearest trees, and made my way along the bluff, to stay concealed from the enemy as long as possible. I got back to my men without taking another shot.

I got off my horse and tied it behind the bluff. I went with a young Cree from bluff to bluff to look for the enemy and get an idea of their numbers. When we arrived at the bluff where I had shot at the scouts, we found a horse with no rider. He had no doubt been knocked off among the trees. It wasn't long before we found the enemy — they were very close. We fired our guns in the direction of the English, and flattened ourselves to the ground. They couldn't tell who had fired the shots or where they came from, so we fired again. This time they saw the smoke and returned fire. We retreated, and when we arrived at the coulee, we found a Sioux who told us one of his people had been killed, and most of the Métis had run off.

I saw Ignace Poitras leading a horse. I followed him a short way and found the runaways. The eight Métis and seven Sioux had advanced about a quarter of a mile. I took them to a coulee east of the bluff where the attack had started, and there were already forty-five Métis. Some of the Métis with me were Antoine Lafontaine, Pierre Sansregret, Edouard Dumont — son of an Assiniboine Métis raised by my Uncle — J.B. Trottier, W. Trottier, young Ladouceur who had no gun but was carrying instead a flag of the virgin, and two young Indians. The seven Sioux fought about fifteen yards from the nine Métis. I had my fourteen-shot repeater, and the young men were giving me their guns to shoot. When we got down to our last seven bullets, I said, "we are going to start a fireline in front of the police." The wind was blowing toward the enemy. We started the fire, and as I was walking the right line to make sure the fire was going, I saw the problem.

I told my men, "we are going to make a sweep, yelling and screaming. March right behind the flames." I always stayed right behind the biggest flames, and when we were about forty yards from the police the fire went out. It was at the edge of a small wet woods. The police were in flight. As we advanced, we found many dead, and no doubt there were many more dead in the underbrush because the water in the little creek was red. We didn't find any rifles or cartridges. The sun had gone down.

The English front line had no doubt already rejoined the troops who were battling the forty-five. "Now that they are a unit," I said, "I am going to get behind them so we can save the forty-five." I wanted to go immediately and scout. But the Sioux refused to follow, so I went alone. I took my horse which had been tied in the bottom of the coulee. I got almost to the edge of the coulee where the enemy was hidden, close to the forty-five. They saw me and fired on me, so I fell back and joined my men.

We went to Calixte Tourond's house to eat. We found all we needed, and killed some chickens and roasted them. Isidore Parenteau arrived with a buggy, two Sioux, and a half-barrel of powder. Soon after two more Sioux arrived on horseback, then Phillippe Gardupuy and Moise Ouellette. They had left when the men making noise behind the fireline were fired on. The Sioux were scouts. Edouard Dumont and Baptiste Boucher came and said eighty horsemen were following them. They had fallen in some snow and gotten their guns wet, so they had gone to Calixte Lafontaine's to dry them. They would be able to shoot better with dry weapons. I told them not to take

Glenbow Archives, Calgary (photo no. NA 4635-1)

Gabriel Dumont with Buffalo Bill's Wild West Show

poor shots, there would be chances for good shots. We moved towards the coulee, and when we got near I went ahead alone. At the edge of the coulee I found two unsaddled Métis horses, saddled them, and returned to give them to my men. I made them scatter, and told them to attack while yelling and shouting. I went down to old Tourond's house, and got back to the Métis without firing a shot. The English were in flight. Even the doctor had abandoned all his bandages and medicines. We found almost two bottles of brandy, which we drank to his health. We decided to start a fire at Tourond's and tend to our wounds. Again we didn't fire at the retreating English: my head wound had reopened and I was just too fatigued to follow them.

Riel stayed at Batoche, and passed the time saying the rosary for the fighters as he listened to the rifle shots. At the end, my brother Edouard said, "I want to go and help them. In our family you never hear rifle shots without there being danger, and I can't stay here and leave them to shoot it out."

The wounded were Challius (also called Charles Thomas) and Charles Carriere — both in the arm, a young Indian in the hand, Boyer in the chest — he died, Cardinal in the neck — he also died, and Pierre Tourond in the thigh. Challius was bothered by his arm wound. People say he would never again show his hand.

Return to Batoche

Riel had sent many wagons to Fish Creek that night. I gave orders to the men on foot to return to Batoche quickly. I stayed on horseback to escort the wagons of wounded. I had already seen four or five mounted men leaving.

But I was bleeding from my head wound and suffering terribly. I was still at Tourond's when I said, "I wish I was well enough to do it myself, but I want the rest of you to stay with the wagons, I'll make it on my own."

After going only half a mile I saw young Jean Dumont and Andre Letendre. I asked "where are you going? I told you to stay with the wounded. You can see I am not well, but if you leave I will have to return." They went back and I went on.

Soon I caught up with the four or five who had deserted earlier. Among them was Napoleon Nault. I was angry with them for leaving. They explained they had left before that order had been given, so they didn't know. I told them I was bleeding a lot and suffering badly, so Napoleon Nault tore a piece of his saddle blanket and bandaged my head. They helped me back to Batoche. We arrived during the night. Someone stabled my horse and I went to sleep at Batoche's house. But Riel called on me to make my report. Then I couldn't sleep. I didn't want to desert my men.

Batoche

The English were camped at my homestead. They burned my house and tore down my stables to reinforce the Northcote and protect it from gunfire. The Métis scouts saw them and we knew that the Northcote was going to come downriver to surround us.

On Saturday they arrived at Batoche before noon. I had placed some Métis on the right side of the river, below the cemetery where the river channel passed a long beach. I thought the Northcote would pass close to the side of the river and almost touch the shore. I had also placed, on the other side of the river, some Métis who could fire on the Northcote, right after it had been fired on from the left. It would be very difficult to get past these two.

I had also given the order to lower the ferry cable, but the men thought it was low enough and didn't move it. The cable barely touched the steamboat. It drifted by. The steamboat anchored a little below Fageron's.

While this was happening, the English had arrived at Caron's. They were trying to turn by Belle Prairie. I sent Michel Dumas and his men to stop the English from fixing the steamboat's chimney, but they were stopped on the height of the bank and their mission was useless.

During the first push, the English tried to sweep through Belle Prairie. They established a machine gun just this side. Once they fired on me and my horse from about one mile, but the bullets fell in front of me. They pulled back at night.

We dug holes near the river bank, the cemetery, and Emmanuel Champagne's. They were about sevent-five yards apart, two or three men in each hole. There were about fifteen men in these pits. The other men were hiding among the small bushes. There were about one hundred and fifty men on this side of the river, and one hundred on the other side. At night we fired at the English as they ate in the strip in front of the old forge. During the night we watched the troops, and the Indians liked to fire on them.

The second day, Middleton worked to establish his fortifications all around his camp, so he could sleep easily. The English started a fire right after breakfast. They controlled the church and cemetery. They moved the machine gun to the small prairie at the top of the trail that ran down into Batoche. It was to the left of the old abandoned trail and to the right of the new trail.

I moved up with my men, crawling along in the small aspens. I told my men, "let me go ahead. I have already been close enough to take a shot in the head — this time they might not miss. When I start shooting, we must take the machine gun, and get down the trail as quickly as possible." I was almost at the place where I could get a good shot away, when my men began to fire. The artillery hadn't started firing yet and reinforcements were arriving, so I withdrew. During the first three days, the English could not move their lines of defense. They sat and didn't move much. One report said that Middleton planned to make us use up our bullets, no doubt on the advice of Father Vegreville.

During the last two days, a Sioux named Joli Corbeau broke his leg at the cemetery. J.B. Boucher, the father, was wounded in the buttock. Armiel Gariepy's wrist was broken and his chest was pierced by the same bullet.

Each night the police returned to their camp, and often there were bullets left on the ground, usually at the foot of a tree, where they had stopped to reload. Often we found machine gun belts which held forty bullets each. These were the same calibre as many of the Métis twelve-shot hunting rifles. We also took the guns of the dead. At the end we had sixty or seventy.

We also came across something very serious — I was amazed when I was shown the exploding balls. We thought it was understood between nations that only mortars could be explosive, as their debris was very destructive. But for a man in combat to be exposed to exploding bullets was to cause a terrible wound and certain death, which was against the basic principles of war. You wanted to score a direct hit, and temporarily disable, but not necessarily kill, the enemy soldiers. A simple bullet wound would disable a man and his wound would get better, while the wound of an exploding ball caused internal wounds and broke bones, and was always deadly. The government troops committed a huge crime against humanity and against the rights of the men of the Métis nation.

On the fourth day around three o'clock the English still hadn't moved past where they had been the day before. The sun was already low when they took Batoche's house. They were pushing in on all sides at once, when they stormed through our front line, they advanced right to the house without stopping. I had not thought of digging the pits until they were coming. In them the men could stay completely secure and hold on right to the end, and then leave without being killed.

This is how they arrived. The English advanced in large battalions, without stopping. They rained bullets on the foxholes: it was a good thing the Métis did not raise their heads to fire. When the English got so close that there was no hope, the Métis tried to fire but were killed instantly.

After the English had entered Batoche's house, which was no longer occupied by the Métis, I continued to resist around there for another half hour. With me were the elder Joseph Vandal, and his nephew Joseph Vandal, the elder Ouellette, Pierre Sansregret, David Tourond, and a young Sioux. We were under Batoche's house. Daniel Ross was wounded in Batoche's house: he yelled to me and the others to come and drag him on to the field of battle.

"Are you dead or alive?" I yelled to him.

"I won't last much longer," answered Ross.

"Then it is good to want to fight on. You might get two deaths instead of one." Daniel Ross was between Batoche's house and Fisher's store.

The English occupied Batoche's house. There was a red curtain in the upstairs window — we didn't often see that.

I kept firing at the curtain to frighten the English, so they would not have time to shoot.

This is when Captain French was shot in the bedroom I had used. He wasn't killed point blank, but was hit in the bedroom just off the passage, and rolled down the stairs, leaving blood stains. He was found at the bottom of the stairs.

Joseph Vandal, the elder, was also wounded at this point. He had both arms broken, one in two places. He was limping, lost his balance, and fell forward. He tried to get up but failed, so I helped him and said, "get out of here. Leave now."

"No," said Vandal. "I prefer to die now that I have two broken arms."

"Go! Go!" I told him, but he wouldn't go, and told me to leave him. So I obliged and left him. I took him across the trail that went down to the crossing, and I went back to fight from Batoche's basement.

A little later we also crossed the trail. The English had already occupied Fisher's store. We fought them from the hill between Fisher's store and his home. It was here that old Ouellette was killed. We found him below the women's tents, which had been abandoned. I put Joseph Vandal in the tent with Tourond and ran on. I was alone now. I found the others a quarter mile further on, towards Emmanuel Champagne's house. They were dead and bayonetted. There was a young wounded Sioux in a wagon near mother Tourond's tent. There was a bullet lodged in his chest, he could not go on. I had to leave him: he was too close to death, bleeding from the mouth. He was the son of Joli Corbeau, who had already been wounded.

After old Ouellette was killed and the English had gone by, we returned to the women's tents. "It is over," I said." But only now that we have held up the English long enough for everyone to escape." I was with Joseph Vandal, Pierre Sansregret, and David Tourond. We met Phillippe Gariepy, John Ross, Carbatte — the son of John Ross, a young English Métis who was the son of Tom Anderson, Hilaire Paternotre, and Henry Smith. Most wanted to leave, but I wanted us to take our last shots. We followed the English in the half-light, and found many bullets as we went.

We followed the river almost to Emmanuel Champagne's. When we got there, I asked Hilaire Paternotre what he wanted to do with the half-barrel of powder he had found. Most of the others had already gone. I wanted him to go and get it, but he wouldn't. So I said to Henry Smith, "you are not afraid, you go and get it. There is no danger. The English aren't there now."

Henry Smith took off his shoes so he could run better. His shoes were hard to run in. He also gave his rifle to John Ross — he wanted someone to carry his shoes but no one would — and John Ross carried his rifle and gave it back when Henry returned.

It was night and we needed to eat. I remembered a Sioux lodge nearby that had had a lot of meat in the last few days. I went and got a leg of dried meat. I came up just this side of Edouard Dumont's where the women had gathered. I gave the calf leg to my wife and told her to share it with the others. Riel's wife was there and so was Riel. It was the last time that I saw him. I heard him say to Madame Riel, "I hope God wants me to live." Everyone was telling them to flee. I wanted to get him a horse so he could get away, if he wanted to.

I said to my wife, "wait for me here." I went to Emmanuel Champagne's stable where I knew there were always horses, but the police had already occupied it. I left without firing on them. I wanted to, but I also wanted to return to my wife and the others.

When I returned she was alone, so I hid her on an island in the river. I went and found a stallion of Batoche's, but he roared and reared so much that I had to tie him in a bluff and go and find another. I met Henry Smith and John Ross' son, who was looking for his father, and Smith wanted his gun back. They told me that Pierriche Parenteau's horses were nearby, so we went to find them. I found a goat, and carried it with me. Henry Smith had the stallion which had gotten loose. We went to Daniel Gariepy's house, where Maxime Lepine had been living. His closest neighbour was Edouard Dumont. We lit a lamp and I brought out two plates, two pots, two knives and forks, and left to get my wife. I found a leavened cake which the police had dropped on the trail. When I got near my wife's hiding place, I tied the stallion and the mare in a bluff nearby. While I was tying the stallion, Pierriche Parenteau's horses galloped by. I thought it was the police. It was now the middle of the night. I went to hide near the bluff with my rifle so I could get the jump on the police, when they passed. First I realized these were free horses, then I realized they were Parenteau's, so I caught another mare and let the stallion go. I put my wife on one of the mares but she had never ridden bareback, so I had to lead her horse with a rope. On the other mare I put a half-bag of flour that I had been carrying when I was leading the the two horses. The stallion followed the two mares and wouldn't leave them. Finally I had to hit him hard with a stick to stop him. We camped at the northeast edge of Belle Prairie.

We spent the morning in the woods where we ate breakfast. I left my wife hidden there and went on foot to find Riel. I went up a bluff going from side to side hiding in the small bluffs. I saw a man hiding near the top of the bluff. It was a Sioux, so I snuck up on him and spoke to him in Sioux. He was very surprised.

I kept looking for Riel, but I couldn't find where he was hiding, so I started calling him very loudly. Jim Short answered me from off to the side, but he wouldn't come up to the prairie, so I went to him. Jim Short told me he had been trying to hide with his horse, but he was going to abandon it because he couldn't hide with it.

"I'll take it myself," I said.

"Take it," he said, and he untied the rope he had around his body and gave it to me.

I went to get the horse and started calling for Riel again. This time, the three young Trottiers answered. They were looking for their mother. There were many Métis horses on the trail so I told them to take them, or the police would.

I returned to my wife with Jim Short's wife. The rest of the Métis were passing through there as they fled, so we followed them. When we arrived at Calixte Lafontaine's we found Emmanuel Champagne's wife in a wagon. She told us that many people who had fled passed there. We went on and found the wife of Baptiste Parenteau, Riel's sister. We followed their tracks and caught up with them near Montour Butte, about ten miles away. There were ten women with Elie Dumont, Pierre Laverdure, and the sons of Pierre Sansregret. We camped with them, and the next day I left one of the mares with the women, and gave the other to Alexandre Fageron, my adopted son. I was going to my father's, when I saw three policemen on the trail escorting some Indians. I had my rifle, as always. They were about three hundred yards away when the Indians saw me and told the police. The police knew my reputation for taking advantage of small enemy patrols, so they sent one of the Indians to talk to me. When he was close enough to speak, I ordered him to stop.

"Are you afraid of me?" asked the Indian.

"Certainly," I said. "How is it that yesterday you fought against the police, and today you help them look for me?"

"You have no reason to fear me."

"Don't come any closer or I will have to shoot you."

The policemen stayed at a distance. They wouldn't come any closer because they knew I wouldn't let them take me alive. I said to the Indian, "I will not lay down my arms — I will fight forever. And the first who comes for me, I will kill." The Indian went back to the police and they left, no doubt to return with reinforcements. But they could not find me.

The Battle of Batoche the Second or Third Day

The machine gun was set up on the prairie in front of the church, between the old and new trails. I wanted to go and kill the gunner, so I told my men to let me approach, and I would shoot him in the head and get rid of the machine gun. But my men at the front took two or three shots at the gun and didn't hit it. So they turned the machine gun in the direction of the fire. The branches were breaking all around me. I ended up crawling under the lowest branches, completely pinned down.

When I was in New York working for Buffalo Bill, a man who knew I was there came and asked for me, and told me, "I fought against you. I was a gunner. I fired the machine gun in front of the church. But that's all over: I am no longer against you. Even then I never shot at you, I only fired in the air, only to scare you. That's what I was hired for.

"I tried hard to kill you, when you were firing above our heads," I said, and told him the story of how I tried to

Glenbow Archives, (Calgary photo no. NA 3432-2)

Gabriel Dumont with his rifle "Le Petit"

put a bullet in his head, but all the branches were breaking around my head in that volley. He was an American from Montana. I was there during the Blackfoot war and if I'd known he was there, I would have killed him.

I went on to my father's, and met J.B. Parenteau who gave me his best horse, which I used to save myself. Moise Ouellette was at my father's. He had a letter for Riel and the others. He gave me the warrant, and I asked if he knew what was in it: "Give it to me and tell me what it says."

"Yes: they promise you justice, if you give yourself up with Riel," answered Moise.

"I will not surrender, but I will keep searching for Riel — not to make him surrender, but escape. If I find him before the law does, I won't let him surrender. I will find him first, Moise.

I did not see Riel again.